Hog Bottom Days

Copyright 2006 by Marcella Norton Wms-Ashe

No part of this book may be reproduced, stored in a retrieval system or transmitted in any form, electronic, mechanical, or by any other means, without written permission of the author.

Library of Congress
Cataloging in Publication Data Under

ISBN: 0-9764198-1-5
ISBN: 978-0-9764198-1-5

Manufactured in the United States of America by
Allecram Publishing @ www.allecrampublishing.com
Telephone: 937-760-6168

Those Hog Bottom Days

Spoken Poetically of
By

Marcella Norton Williams-Ashe

Illustrated by Anthony Williams, Jr.

Editing and Page Layout by Jeanese Ray

of

Ivy Branch Designs

Introduction of the Author

Marcella Norton Williams-Ashe was born and lived in Dayton, Ohio her entire life. Being an inspired poet, she started her career by writing poetically her book of poetry, *When The Red Brick Road Turned Yellow*. This book is an Authorhouse publication. Marcella has multiple writing skills which has led her to self- publishing a children's book 'Granny Says". She is presently doing business as Allecram Publishing.

The book, *Those Hog Bottom Days spoken of Poetically,* shows how people, where she grew up, enjoyed their way of life by sharing and caring in their community. Community obligation was a privilege that carried a realness.

The author has tried to recapture, poetically, the meanings as well as the feelings reflected by her years while growing up in the community known as Hog Bottom.

Dedication

I am dedicating this book to my Hog Bottom family. This small revelation of what community growth was like earlier may inspire some of the younger generation to confront, not the old equipment that was used; but to view the values shared.

To my beautiful children and their wives Timothy La Shawn and Sheila Williams, Anthony and Asia Williams Jr.

To my mother and father; Mr. and Mrs. Clarence Norton Sr.

To my grandmothers who showed much love to everyone's children; Mrs. Irene Nelloms and Mrs. Gladys Norton. To my grandfathers who were the ones who held the fort down; Mr. Frank Nelloms and Mr. Art Norton. To Uncle and Aunt Jethro Nelson.

To my brothers and sisters Pastor Clarence and Frances Norton Jr.; Pastor Carl and Annie Norton Sr., and Timothy Norton. To my only sister and her husband, Ryan and Vickie L. Shaw

God has blessed me with yet a beautiful extended family. My beloved husband James L. Ashe Sr. James and Monica Ashe Jr. Jeanese Ashe, Darnell Ashe, Dionne R. Ashe, Jason L. and Chanell Ashe, Jeffrey A. and Davion Ashe.

Many, aunts, uncles, and cousins are my source of strength. This book is dedicated to you for your unending support. To my family in Dallas, Texas and Homer, Louisiana for pushing me on.

A special dedication to the Newspaper pushers that resided in Hog Bottom. To my dear cousin, Albert Jones, for track and field. Gerald McKee for basketball, and to Kenneth Hoskins for football. To Rosa Melson who had to be the fastest girl in track, because she beat me running and I was pretty fast.

Acknowledgments

I would like to thank my friends from this Hog Bottom community for caring and sharing in this community development. I am a product of Hog Bottom, and would like to thank neighbors and friends for a job well done. It would be impossible for me to include everyone who played a part In Hog Bottom Days into my book. You, my friends, know that you were there and for this I Thank You All.

I would like to acknowledge Mrs. Wendy H. Beckman and Jeanese Ray, for editing my work. Thank you for your love and patience.

I would like to acknowledge those from my General Motors family and Valerie Coleman for encouraging me to go on.

To Mr. Anthony Williams Jr. my illustrator, my beloved son who makes illustrating work just the way I want it.

To Jeanese Ray of Ivy Branch Designs for the page layout.

To my Printers Book Masters.

If I overlooked anyone it was not intentional and you are not left out. Thank you for being a part of me.

Contents

What is Hog Bottom 1

Those Hog Bottom Days 3

Memoir of the People of Hog Bottom 8

Fashion 10

Patchwork of Hog Bottom 12

A Tribute to Fathers & Mothers
   of Hog Bottom 15

His Story 17

Her Story 19

Hog Bottom Contributors 21

Memoirs of Miami Chapel School 22

Hog Bottom's Harold Mitchell 24

Purpose and Inspiration 26

Photographs -- From Then to Now 29

Poetry Contributions
   From People of Hog Bottom 45

Reflections 62

What Is Hog Bottom?

Hog Bottom is the name given, by who in the heck knows, to a community on the west side of Dayton Ohio, where the people lived and worked together; and the neighbors actually watched the children there, grow.

It is really too bad that only memories are left in the hearts and accomplishments of the people that knew; that the life before us would make Hog Bottom just our point of view.

Those Hog Bottom Days

And Those Were Hog Bottom Days

It feels good remembering the days when a petticoat graced a girl's skirt. It made the hogs happy when the rainwater turned the streets into dirt.

If you came along when the rain poured and would not stop; you would see hogs running in the mud slop. Those were the good old days, everybody had some good days.

In Hog Bottom we thought that we were rich. People worked with each other, bending backwards to watch for the children that needed the switch*.

There was the iceman that brought ice for the icebox that kept our food cold. The milkman brought eggs and butter he sold.
There was a man that picked up our dirty Sunday clothes, with a promise to have everything back in twenty-four hours pressed and fold.

There were doctors that made house calls, and neighbors that would tell your parents how often you would fall, when you were in front of their house, playing ball.

On Sundays to church the entire family went; not like today when just the children are sent. Aunts, uncles and cousins made Sundays a rest day. On this day no one was allowed to go outside to play.

Almost everyone owned a piece of land; planting and preparing a garden that required everyone's hands. When the garden was finished growing, the neighbors would share. There was canning and preserving with mason jars everywhere.

The steel gray tub was where we bathed* -- twice in the water because the first water was saved. We also left our doors opened to the outside in case a relative wanted to come in. It could also be a neighbor coming in. A neighbor was not just a neighbor -- a neighbor was always considered a friend.

And we must never forget the man with the coal. Coal that fed our old pot bellied stove. This stove kept our entire house warm and not very hot. It sure filled in when the quilt would miss a spot.

There was this unusual man pulling a little red wagon, selling and yelling 'ice cream, candy--and a smile'. We called him Mr. Happy. He rested only for a little while. We followed him around. We wanted to know where he lived; he was our childhood character but not a clue would he give.

We had a man that delivered watermelons; those melons with the jet black seeds. The bread man delivered, and so did the man with spices and vanilla flavor and liniment for bad knees.

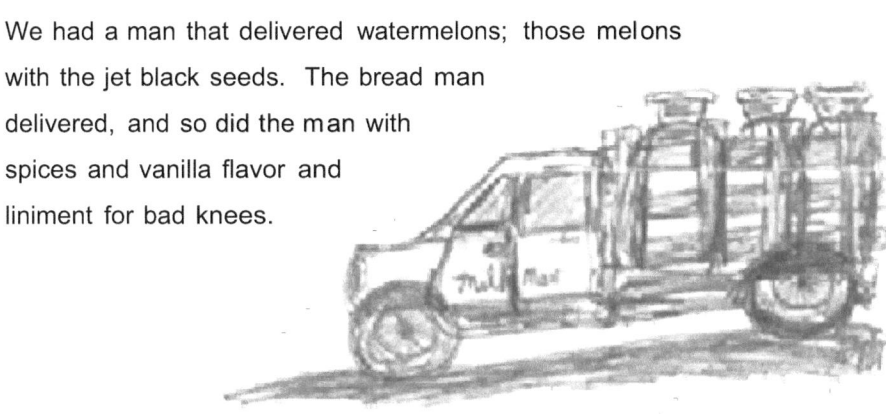

A road that ran right down the middle of it all. There was drag racing in cars. There were no sidewalks; there were just the trees that lined a street named Richley.

Our old High School now stands on the hog's hill afar. A high school rebuilt in the honor of Paul Laurence Dunbar.

When I came along the History of Hog Bottom was nearly made. The hogs were gone; the stories are just some of the memories I have saved.

In the year 2004, some things happened on the old hog's floor. A Senator came to what used to be our Hog Bottom. This Senator was running for President of our country. He was surrounded by famous movie stars standing on a platform, while making his speech just above where our pigs were born.

I was so honored to see Judge Joe Brown and LaVar Burton, BeBe Winans and more. There was live entertainment almost in my aunt and uncle's front door.

All of our hogs are long gone, but people just won't leave the Hog Bottom area alone.

Good Night!

---

*switch - a small branch from a tree used to make children do what they were told.
*bathed - taking a bath but in a tub.

Memoirs Of The People That Owned The Hog Farm

Mr. and Mrs. Jacob Lane Bennett

Bought the farm in 1948

Sold the farm to the Dayton Board of Education in 1960

Owned and ran one of our neighborhood stores

Owned Hog Bottom's first Night Club, Jabená.

Jacob and Mary Bennett

The memories of walking to school, and not having to wait for a bus, stopping on our way to school at the neighborhood store.
The amount of money we had did not really matter, if the lady behind the counter said, "you have had enough you may have no more."

In this era, families were really organized. Fathers stood by mother's side. Mealtime was shared with the entire household at the same time. Everyone watched the same TV show. This part of our life had to be one of a kind.

There was a lady truant officer named Mrs. Green. She managed to keep a curfew for the juveniles behind the Hog Bottom fence, or you would suffer a severe consequence.

We were sorta' glad the hogs would soon move.
We needed the new high school in our neighborhood.

The Hog Bottom Days were nearly over when
I came along. I do remember how we transcend
From one era to another in changing the style of
clothes, that we wore.

Fashion

Kissing boys in those days did not really matter,
as long as you could wear the boy's letter on your sweater.

If you had problems seeing yourself to your school classes, just grab
yourself a pair of granny glasses.

The fabric, that our clothes were made from, must have been super strong to
endure all the washboard rubbing and clothesline drying in the sun.

People in Hog Bottom did keep up with the trends. I
remember my brother wearing a cap made of coon skin.

I do not know if all fashions are so correct; we thought so
much of our sweater called a turtleneck.

Mothers looked like women that aimed to please,
working in modest clothing that covered their knees.

All good things must come to some end.
We move forward to another fashion trend.

Platform shoes, bell bottomed pants, and giant Afros.
Men could wear pink clothes and no one turned up their nose.

The Beatles and the bangs that covered half of your face.
Still very little juvenile crime in our place.

Then you see the psychedelic prints, and shirts that were tie dyed, and
those that saw birds that flew past in the sky.

Hog Bottom had to progress and the hogs could not stay,
for we could not grow with mud slop in our way.

Camps, Ross, Sledge, Henderson, Thomas, Nelson, White, Dorsey, Crowder, Thompson, Burke, Henderson, Jackson, Simms, Cortner, Weaver, Randolph, Wood, Curry, Nellom, Black, Johnson, Allen, Shackleford, McMahon, Lewis, Ford, Armstrong, Mitchell, Wesson, Armstrong, Norton, Jones, Johnson, Barnes, Hill, McGill, Brown, Ross, Milton, Daddy-O, Blackshear, Floyd, Austin, McKee, Cheetams, Henry, Dillard, Bennett, Kirksey, Heard, Reynolds, Chandler, Robinson, Adams, Calwell, Edwards, Johnson, Stone, Melson, Broadus, Nelms

"The uncharted but not forgotten people that refused to let unsuitable situations dominate their lives"

Hog Bottom located in the West side of Dayton, Ohio.
I grew up straddling the mid fifties and the sixties.
I am a baby boomer who cherishes the memories.

Patch Work of Hog Bottom

Remembering when mistakes were corrected by neighbors and family friends.

Pieces and patches of land made growing dinner from your garden, a master plan.

Mom and Dad were certainly a team.
Go against one and the other would destroy your dream.

When being a virgin meant wearing a virgin pin.
Doing the twist was a sin.

So, when there was time to kill;
I would read books like "The Power of Positive Thinking" by Norman Vincent Peale.

Moving forward only to look back at our human errors as being small mistakes.

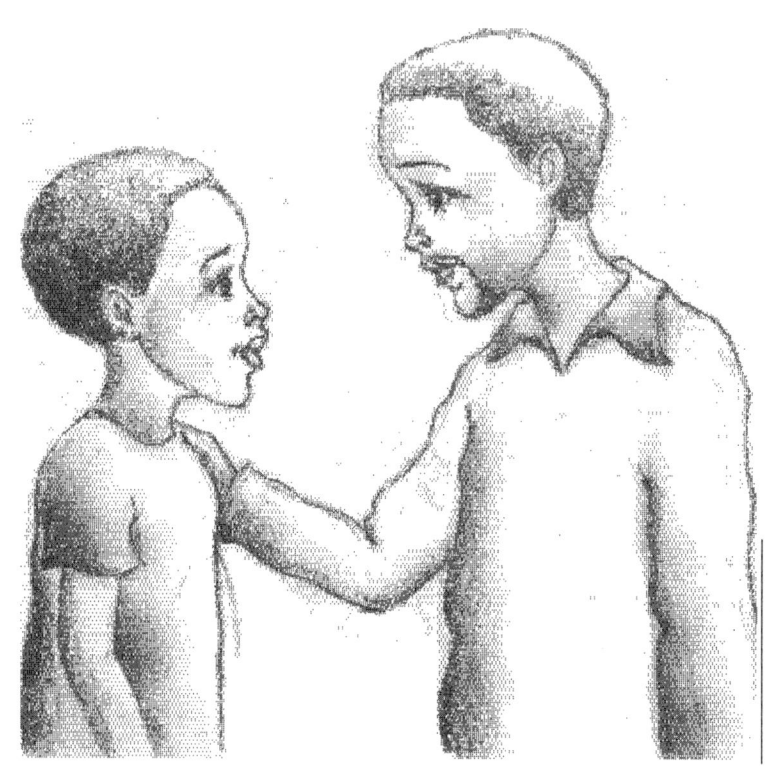

His Story

*There was nothing left to reveal about myself
She stood like a tower in the middle of my destiny until there
was absolutely nothing left. Since my spirit has drained* inwardly
and the barriers that she has built left me just a stepping stone,
that I somehow used as a bridge. My situation has now become
a part of her possessions. And now I struggle because the
power and the strength that remained in her had been her
secret until the unveiling of myself, but I too possess a
secret to shield. I placed myself in God's
will. And all of those
biblical men and men that live in past history
I missed the revelation of how we are placed in such a
rewarding thrill. I was created in God's image so I do not need
to hide the strength given *to me. -It is only countdown time until the
world will see, that the power to rule will remain inside of me. I will honor
and respect what opposes me. And of all the things that have been told
to me, I know that God also holds me.*

Her Story

I am the inventor, with little evidence in my possession as I crawled around on uncultivated earth, making all of the necessary alterations; leaving trails of paper often used to buy and sell in some marketplace. I will hide my title of mobility in the coat of the one so in charge of what I need to wear. Casting a shimmer of light to smear what I need to read. I am determined to continue an ended journey, that only death can in the defeat of stopping my finished line conquest. Injured and sometimes outraged because of my favorable results; looking for master approval, diving in to absorb the accomplishments, placing myself at their mercy and slowing my struggle. I will walk maybe even run a little faster, habits leave conditions, moldy and unprepared for the evaluation. Later in time I will gather my title of respect. To execute the unconnected, finding love and hidden answers on the lower levels, bringing out what should have never started to the rightful end.

"Death and Life are in the power of the tongue"
Proverbs 18:21

Sharing the limited potentials of staying fair, I want to recognize all of the business that brought us together as a community as I remember them.

The Avenue Grill
Bell's Drug Store
Bell's Grocery Store
Bennett's Store
B&D Records
Borden Milk
Bowman's Funeral Home Cheetams
Carry Out
Coal Man
Dayton Speedway
Happy Days Cleaners
Ice Man
J & W Party Supply
King Solomon's Church
Lawson's Dairy
Louise Troy School

Mann's Store

McLin Funeral Home

Miami Chapel School

Mitchell's Grocery (shoe shine shop in the back)

Ohio Ice Cream Truck

Pantorium Cleaners

Prayer Garden Church

Raleigh Man

Ren'sMarket

Rexall's Drug Store

Shaw Cleaners

Sunset Drive-In

Valley Grove Church

Wogaman Elementary School

Memoirs of Miami Chapel Elementary School

We were obedient and well trained even in our elementary school system. The girls were taught to sew an apron and some made a skirt or blouse. We knew how to darn a sock or put a button back in place. Home Economics had a real sound effect on all of us.

The boys were taught wood shop and learned how to make windmills and other structures from wood. We were taught to cherish the value in what we were doing.

We had one lady truant officer, Mrs. Green, who managed the whole Hog Bottom area without a problem of keeping order. You see, we were taught and learned to demonstrate discipline when we did not see the value in what our parents had to say.

My seventh grade teacher, Mr. Scott, stands out most of all. Mr. Scott was our seventh grade math teacher. He was a very authoritative person in our lives, and did not tolerate disobedience. He swung a big paddle with lots of holes in the paddle. He would discipline anyone of us, girls *and* boys, on the padded part of our body without parental permission. I really appreciate and respect the moral results that are within me because of the stand the people in charge took.

Miami Chapel School front entrance
Built in 1952

Hog Bottom's Harold Mitchell

Harold Mitchell, a Hog Bottom native, was employed by Mr. Louis Botwin, store owner in Dayton's west side at the young age of 14. Mr. Mitchell worked for the Botwins until he was 24 years old. During his entire 10 years of employment, he never missed a day of work.

Being very smart about the business, Harold asked his boss about a Junior Partnership at the store where he was employed. Unfortunately, he was turned down by the owner.

The owner did sell to another one of Hog Bottom's business entrepreneurs, Mr. Halls. In the one month that Harold worked for the new manager He once again made the offer for partnership in the business. This time the new manager, Mr. Hall, made Harold an offer; stating that if he could handle the stock expense he could run the store under the original name. Harold sought financial support from a financial institution in the area. He was turned down by the bank, but he supported by continued banking. Harold married a wonderful woman named Jeanette, from North Carolina, who promised to support his dream of buying the store. Having her to back him up for any support that he would need, he managed to buy the stock, from his savings to later purchase the store at 1100 Randolph in 1950 at the age of twenty-four.

Mr. Mitchell absorbed all of the customers that were going to Botwin's new store and paid Mr. Hall every two weeks for the fixtures that remained with the store, until they were paid off. He was finally able to place his name on the business which became Mitchell's Market. Employee, Mrs. Anna M. Hill was a great support in running the Mitchell Market business. This employee worked faithfully and covered all areas in assisting with the running of the store. Mr. Mitchell moved from this location in 1960. Before the Urban Renewal took over, a man named Mr. Henry, also known as "Daddy-O", took over the store for about a year. Mr. Henry later moved to the Germantown location.

One of Mr. Harold Mitchell's hobbies has been amateur radio, since 1978. He is involved in health and welfare as chair person, the Scholarship Fund Director of 75. Harold used to enjoy motorcycle riding.

Mr. Harold Mitchell's advise to the children of this era:
"Preserve your dreams. Obstacles will make you tough enough to obtain everything. Keep perusing your dreams. If you can dream it and believe it, then you can achieve it."

Purpose and Inspiration

It is my fault that I am sad and irritable.
It is my fault that I feel you are not where you want me to be? It is
not my fault that I am not anger free.
There is anger and violence surrounding me every where I go and this is
something that you already know.

It is not the hardness of my rock that
makes my mountain hard to climb.
It is the softness of my heart that keeps
the children of tomorrow on my mind.

Confused thinking, thoughts of death and suicide.
Needing a guided hand and a fatherly smile.
Why did you stop being the host; in this new age day when
moms need dads the most.
And you stand there muttering, "What is the world coming to?"
When you know the world started from inside of you.

Photographs From Then to Now

Home of the Blackshears - Then
(Sue & Lillie)

The Blackshear home – Now
(Photos donated by Willis Blackshear)

George and Beatrice Thomas
(Photo donated by grandson, Bill)

Miami Chapel School (back)

Miami Chapel School (front)

Reconstruction of Wogamon Elementary School

Newly renovated Wogamon Elementary School

Front view of Louise Troy Elementary School

The street (Dennison) where I grew up

Della Street, in Hog Bottom, as it looks today

Germantown Street is the hill that led to our entertainment
(The Sunset Drive-In and the Dayton Speedway)

Haller Avenue

The fields where the hogs used to kick up the mud slop

This is how the fields look today

B & D Records

Bell's Drug Store

Shaw's Cleaners, (above & below) is a black owned business

Madden Hills is a part of what used to be
Hog Bottom (above & below)

This is how Richley looks today

Homes built by my late uncle Jethro Nelson

Paul Laurence Dunbar High School (above)
Sits right on the previously hog bottom floor

Contributions from the Poets

# of Hog Bottom

Hog Bottom Pride

Let us reminisce as we go back: recalling fond
memories with some of the facts.
A time where innocence was definitely clear,
everyone was your family and there was not much to fear. We
all had moments of being naughty or nice,
being mischievous three times twice. We did
nothing to alarm or cause anyone harm.

We grew up innocently with a childlike charm. And like
most children, we would fuss and fight. This did not last
very long; because we soon forgot
who was wrong or right. A message we would send…
forget the dumb fight and remain friends.

We did not let much get in our way, because it did not hurt to
step aside. It did not hurt our Hog Bottom Pride. Yes, we were
the children of Hog Bottom and very proud to be, for being
here meant freedom, and we were free. Happy and free from
worldly strife,
and the struggling cares of life.

We found pleasure in the simple little things--rolling a tire or playing roses around the ring. We made our go-carts, we played four square too. Playing dodge ball in the streets was nothing new.

We were busy like bees, chattering with a buzz,
Calling out to each other, "How Ya Doing Cuz"
We could walk throughout our neighborhood at any time, night or day, and peacefully play. There were no drive-by shootings or hoodlums hanging around. This was our Hog Bottom… our side of town.

We can not paint this picture perfect, because perfect does not exist anywhere. The world will always have problems and we were keenly aware.

We lived in Hog Bottom and everyone knew that we had Hog Bottom Pride. We were the few.

This place was a special place where we could freely roam. It held our laughter, our freedom. It was our home.

We still yearn and learn from the good old days in Hog Bottom. Sadly, though others have left and some have died. But what a joy to live and tell others about the Hog Bottom Pride.

Martha A. Jones Gomez

Vestibule

Shaded with the color chalky white balls of ivy
Set aside for one to consecrate
in willingness to unproposed boldness.

Walking shoulder to shoulder,
not touching the walls of coldness.

Shimmers of a weak but guiding light
came slightly into our view.

Guidance for direction will leave a
memorandum to those concerned.

One by one all doors are closed,
a book of your efforts are earned.

Marcella Norton Wms-Ashe

The Hummingbird and the Butterfly

The hummingbird asked the butterfly about
the scent of the hogs in the air, hopscotch and
a game called four square.

I remember the children, using energy without a care,
jumping up and down, backwards and forward,
zig-zagging and cart wheeling in mid air.

The butterfly wanted to know more about the boys
humming under the street lights, until the girls went
home, out of the boys' sight.

I know freedom says the butterfly. I survived a
struggle from my cocoon. The children today have
a new freedom from yesterday's room.

What happened to hide and seek: It appears the children
are seeking a place to hide and weep. We must turn
to fly away from this day. The beauty of yesterday
is turning gray.

I am just a small hummingbird. I know the weight a flower
can bear. Each child will need a loving push, or the flower
will tear.

Flowers that we once knew are the seeds of the people
below. We must reclaim their efforts; stir up the ground for a
new seed to grow.

We will return again to this place, one day when the smell of
flowers will cover the hog's scent. Loving your neighbors
will be the main event.

Hog Bottom
(by Richley)

Straight as an arrow goes Richley Drive
path memories, ...oh boy!
From scrap yards, educational Chapels of
Miami; later joined by the Louise of Troy
Landfills and gravel hills, stored, with young
children crossing grassy fields
A gurgling creek streaming past those resting in
Green Castle's Estate separating Jacob's house, Mary's
store, and the Bennett's farm to piggery gates. Many
stories are long, some cut short;
And a few, plain forgotten
But, Frizell, Randolph, Dennison, to Haller the
directions to Hog Bottom.

Clarence Norton

Thoughts Of Sunflowers

With sunshine amaranthine glowing
silky

Presented as lifting a reality to
permeate

Dreams with knowledge enfolding
beyond
myself

Marcella Norton Wms-Ashe

Nothing That I Can Feel

The clouds above are laying lazily in the sky
There is a smell of cologne in the daily rush.
The mirror stared at me not saying much.
The process of the caterpillar's loom
will sport a silk suit all too soon.
Those that lay silently underground,
untouchable, hidden under the brown.
Sighing, crying, laughing, the screaming,
discovering the sounds of something new.
The sweat on mother's brow when I was born,
laughing flashing and the sky was torn.
From the sun something lovely and warm I drew,
when my hands are folded with nothing to do.
You have touched me, without me
touching you.

Marcella Norton Williams-Ashe

Sister Dear

It's a girl! They all did cheer though
my reign lasted but a year then came
you my sister dear. And ever since it
was quite clear, that I would never be
alone
and without you I'd have never known
how to share my very own
and help each other as we have grown.

We used to fuss and sometimes fight,
determined to be the one who's right.
Matching outfits – we were a sight
in our ponytails and our colored tights.
The time we cut each other's hair
and fought over the "pink elephant" underwear. We
sometimes did not like to share
we did not care – it wasn't fair.

Oh, how quickly time has flown and
who would have ever known.
Now, sister dear, that we have grown,
and both have children of our own. All
the memories through the years,
I think of the laughter and the tears.
Whether you are far or near
you'll always be my sister dear.

Ivy Branch

God's Garden

God blessed the ground on which we played.

A flower has grown from each house, a bouquet has

been made.

In God's garden there are flowers that

only God can name.

These are usually man's unnoticed

and unclaimed..

In God's garden there is hard work, put into making things grow.

The hoe that moves the dirt makes the row.

When the work was done and you looked unclean; wishing that

no one asked where you have been.

The purpose for this garden remain all

new; for the watering

of this garden are your tears of despair, in

the morning dew.

And some wonder why I love God when I seem alone

I answer them this way "I am not alone, I

am just a little windblown.

He has made all of the wonders of the world,

even the garden for everyone to see.

I am so thankful that

he has chosen me.

      Marcella Norton Wms-Ashe

Children Of Today

There are four very important things I want you to know,

This will water your soil as you grow.

My little brothers and sisters stop and think,

and rest your mind a little while.

There is some damage done when you turn your television dial.

Those you see on television are not living in poverty;

so please do not try to play their part.

They are paid to play act from the very start.

There are the east and the west, south and the north;

from the four corners of the earth women will give birth.

Read, so that you may learn that wisdom is a kind of

energy that you cannot burn.

God made nature obey. Follow your hearts

my little ones because God made you that way.

Marcella Norton Wms-Ashe

Framed Memories

Rims
Of Gold

Hugs
Protective Lights

Living
To Cover

Soiled
Places

Peeling
Colors, of the Past

Clarence Norton, Jr.

God Remembers
(Sparrow)

A small pile of bones that feathers once raced
the spirit of song
God gifted and graced.

Retired reaper of the green and brown, hunter of the blue,
which quietly slept with moon and stars,
an early hopper of dew.

A prey for nine lives and wise-eyed hawks
it sojourned paths through,
living pioneered thoughts.

But when toils of the flighty claimed it's win
and health of the well did not depend
God cuddled the little song in memories:
A tune that others soon forgot.

Clarence Norton, Jr.

When Enough Is Not Enough

The horrendous explosion of premeditation of killing one another.
Shattering dreams, dismissing the hugs and love of a sister or brother.

Breaking the chains that hold onto our children's hands.
Allowing forgiveness to unfold with peace to make love a demand.

So we now lay education on the table to search for what is
missing.

The Adam Olympics keeps our children running with the crawling and
evil hissing.

Hog Bottom was our neighborhood.
Every community should love our broken children as God would.

Enough is not enough because one race is won.
Let's celebrate the race of our children, each and every one.

Marcella Norton Wms-Ashe

God's Eyes

The lifestyles and the concepts were global in our time. Good
times just kept kicking the hard times around.
I will always cherish the grandmothers of long ago.
Grandmothers were the neighbors you wanted to know.

When our fathers and mothers were asleep,
God kept on watching our Hog bottom family.
When God turned the west side of Dayton black with the dark; The
moon and the stars were a reflection of
God's eyes on our Hog Bottom Park.
No one needed to see that we were God's priority.

Marcella Norton Wms-Ashe

He Knew

Those constrained were found healed with time

Enduring a life with a never ending love vine

Shielding death from those with a low self esteem

Adding without thought foolish conversation

To expose those with voiceless imagination,

To crashing unspoken dreams.

He knew they were feelings;

weakness was not knowing what to do.

Gaining strength unprepared was just another's point of view

A celebrated new spirit released into our universe

New improvements to our old mistakes

God knew from the beginning, that anything

You start would gather an ending

Marcella Norton Wms-Ashe

Write Your Reflections

Anthony Williams Jr. was born February 9, 1973. He is a Patterson Co-op graduate. Anthony has worked in photography, graphic arts designs, artwork on book covers and Page lay-outs.

Anthony also provides the transportation for Mt Zion Transformation Ministries by driving the church bus. He is also the church Y.P.W.W. youth president. Anthony is a faithful husband to Asia and father to one son. A man with many hats and talents is Mr. Anthony Williams Jr.

Anthony is the illustrator of the designs for the book Granny Says. He carefully brought Granny and each illustration in the book to life. He is gifted and a great graphic artist.

Mrs. Williams says her books would not come alive without him. Anthony's brother Timothy Williams is also an artist.

Anthony is great at providing for you whatever you ask of him in the field of artwork. Examples of his work are found in Granny Says and Those Hog Bottom Days. The covers of all of Mrs. Ashe's books are works of working together to make the books that grace your shelves. Mrs. Ashe has accredited Mr. Williams as her helping hand.

Ivy Jeanese Ray is a native of Hampton, Virginia who joined the Dayton, Ohio community in 1990. Since relocating to Dayton, she has worked as the Registrar of Management Training at NCR Corporation and L. M. Berry Company. Ivy has also spent several years as a trainer in Computer Literacy and Microsoft Programs, for the Edgemont Neighborhood Coalition, and the Dayton Urban League.

Ivy is the owner of Ivy Branch Designs which has provided over 20 years of graphic design and technical editing services to numerous companies, election campaigns, and individuals in the Miami Valley area and across the nation.

An important aspect of her life is family -- her husband, Clarence A. Ray, III, and two sons, Clarence (Anthony) Ray, IV and Christopher Ray.

More Books By Marcella Norton Williams-Ashe

Allecram Publishing Dayton,
Ohio 45405
www.allecrampublishing.com
marcellaashe@sbcglobal.net
937-760-6168

ISBN 0-9764198-0-7

'Granny Says'

A delightful Bible-based children's book of alphabetically arranged stories containing scripture references, for ages 1-7. Wonderfully done with colorful illustrations

Excerpt:
L is for Love – Jesus loved the little children. Jesus blessed the children too. Mark 10:13-16

My Granny says, "God has promised children a long life on this earth if they obey their parents."
Ephesians 6:2-3

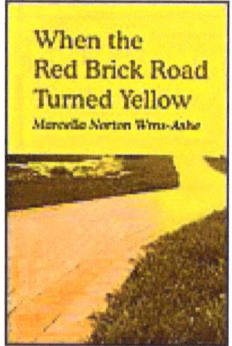

ISBN 1-4140-0669-1

'When the Red Brick Road Turned Yellow'

This collection of thought provoking poetry is warm and inspiring.

Excerpt - *When the Red Brick Road Turned Yellow*:

The treasure is in the brick, and the color does not matter. She walked the red but pleasured the yellow. She journeyed across her life's meadows and found her roads to be moist and shallow. She cried...

www.ingramcontent.com/pod-product-compliance
Lightning Source LLC
Chambersburg PA
CBHW042002150426
43194CB00002B/93